I0160712

Australian Biographical Monographs

26

Australian Biographical Monographs

Series Editor: Scott Prasser

Previous Volumes

Australian Biographical Monographs

26

Paul Hasluck

Anne Henderson

Connor Court Publishing

Australian Biographical Monographs 26
Anne Henderson
Published in 2025 by Connor Court Publishing Pty Ltd

Connor Court Publishing Pty Ltd
PO Box 7257
Redland Bay QLD 4165
sales@connorcourt.com
www.connorcourt.com

Printed in Australia

ISBN: 9781923568044

Front Cover Photograph: Getty Images.

In short, I've listened to the House, throughout a year
Heard cries of "Rubbish", "Order" and "Hear, hear"
With rising pressure and hardening party cries
I've heard a little truth and many lies.
But never heard, though listening late and long,
"I beg your pardon" and "Perhaps I may be wrong".

- Paul Hasluck, "Words Unheard are Sweeter"[1]

Australian Biographical Monographs

Series overview

The Connor Court Publishing's *Australian Biographical Series* on past leading Australian political leaders and other important figures seeks to provide an overview for those who are unfamiliar with the subject and to highlight the person's particular importance, controversies and contributions to Australia's progress.

The monographs are scholarly rather than academic in focus placing emphasis on a clear narrative, but with careful attention to referencing to ensure views expressed are supported by appropriate sources and evidence.

The Series was initiated because of the decline in the study of Australian history at our schools and universities and the consequential lack of knowledge or even worse, distorted views of some of Australia's leading figures who deserve to be remembered, understood for both their achievements, and as each volume also highlights, their flaws.

The last full biography of Neville Wran, Labor Premier of New South Wales from 1976 to 1986, was by two journalists, one who had worked for him and another who reported on his government at the time. A celebratory edited collection and a chapter in a book on Premiers by a Wran confidant followed a decade later. These publications gave important insights into Wran and his government. Now, over three decades since the Wran era ended, this new monograph by Dr David Clune OAM provides a timely reassessment of Wran and his government less influenced by personal loyalties or reporting on immediate events. Dr Clune, long-time Manager of the New South Wales Parliament's Research Service and the Parliament's Historian, brings a wealth of knowledge to consider from a more long-term perspective if Neville Wran was New South Wales' most impressive premier of the 20th Century.

Introduction

I began work at the New South Wales Parliament on 2 December 1974. By chance, I was in the visitors' gallery soon after for Premier Bob Askin's last day in the Legislative Assembly.

I remember clearly the buzz of excitement that emanated from Neville Wran's office when he was Leader of the Opposition. I was on the parliamentary staff for his years as Premier. It was, even for an onlooker like me, an exhilarating time. I have subsequently written about Wran in various publications (listed in the Select Bibliography). I have drawn on these for this biography. Other basic sources are: *The Wran Model* edited by Ernie Chaples, Helen Nelson, and Ken Turner; Brian Dale, *Ascent to Power: Wran and the Media*; Mike Steketee and Milton Cockburn's *Wran: An Unauthorised Biography*; *The Wran Era*, edited by Troy Bramston. Articles in Rodney Cavalier's *Southern Highlands Newsletter* are a primary source.

I have endeavoured, where possible, to tell Wran's story using the voices of close participants. I have been fortunate to have the assistance of a number of those who have first-hand knowledge of the era: Rodney Cavalier, Milton Cockburn, Brian Dale and Terry Sheahan. I would also like to acknowledge the help of Nick Greiner and Gary Sturgess. My sincere thanks to them all. The responsibility for errors, omissions and misinterpretations remains my own.

With his unrivalled accuracy and expertise, Antony Green calculated the election results in Appendix Two, on which all election figures in the text are based.

At Connor Court, Scott Prasser was a helpful and supportive editor and Anthony Cappello displayed his usual professionalism.

David Clune

July 2020

"*Balmain boys don't cry. We're too vulgar, too common for that. But if you prick us with a pin, we bleed like anyone else.*"

-- Speech to ALP Annual Conference, June 1983

Early career[1]

Neville Kenneth Wran was born on 11 October 1926 in Balmain in inner Sydney, the youngest of the eight children of Joseph and Lillian. A heavily industrialised area, Balmain was hit hard by the Depression in Wran's childhood. His father, originally a merchant seaman, struggled to find work. Although in later years he made much of his Balmain origins, when Neville was ten the Wrans moved to nearby Five Dock, a more middle-class suburb. With tireless energy and resourcefulness, Lilly educated and provided for her children and instilled in them conventional standards of respectability. Neville was more scholarly than sporting, a considerable handicap in traditional Balmain. He compensated with personal charm and quick-wittedness.

Educated at Nicholson Street Public School and Drummoyne High, Neville won a scholarship to the selective Fort Street for his final two years of high school. He excelled at debating and acting and briefly considered a career on the stage before enrolling in law at Sydney University in 1944. Wran had an affinity for his legal studies and worked hard at them. The social milieu of the University also suited him. He was popular, particularly with female students, and acquired a taste for the sophisticated life. He became close friends with a fellow law student, Bill Waterhouse of the well-known book-making family, working as a runner for Waterhouse and enjoying Sydney night-life with him. Wran continued to act and debate and wrote rather smug gossip articles for the student newspaper, *Honi Soit*. He showed no interest in Labor or radical politics and was, in fact, briefly a member of the University Liberal Club. Wran graduated LLB with second class honours in 1948.

Wran was employed by the firm of Bartier, Perry and Purcell in 1947, first as an articled clerk then a solicitor. When he was 20, he married Marcia Oliver, whose divorce his firm was handling. He adopted her son, Glenn. They had a daughter, Kim. The marriage ended in divorce and Wran married Jill Hickson in 1976. They had a daughter, Harriet, and son, Hugo.

Wran had a productive and prosperous decade with Bartier, Perry and Purcell and could have gone on to become a senior partner. Instead, he chose the riskier course of going to the Bar, slowly building a successful practice.

Gerry Peacocke, later a Country Party MP and minister, was a solicitor in Dubbo in central western NSW who often briefed Wran. He has given this description of him in action: "He had a very persuasive manner with juries. He was not flamboyant: he adopted almost a conversational tone. Neville understood people and how to get to them. His judgment of people was very perceptive. He had an innate ability to communicate with ordinary people ..."[2] Wran also had the ability to master the details of a brief rapidly, enormous reserves of energy, a fierce competitiveness, a hunger to succeed, and a certain ruthlessness. All of this propelled him into the elite of Sydney barristers. He became a Queen's Counsel (QC) in 1968.

Thanks to his success at the Bar, Wran had an expensive home in the exclusive Sydney suburb of Darling Point and drove a Jaguar. Nonetheless, he spiced up his language with profanities, vulgar analogies and working class expressions. Wran revelled in a cosmopolitan lifestyle and colourful company. He had a volatile personality: although often warm and charming he could explode into tirades of vile, expletive-laced abuse. He was also an unforgiving enemy.

Wran practised increasingly in industrial law. This led him towards Labor politics. Two legal friends from that time were future Whitlam Government ministers, Lionel Murphy and Jim McClelland. Another Labor lawyer, leading barrister Jack Sweeney, befriended Wran and gave him *entrée* into the complex but lucrative field of trade union briefs. These came from both the left and right.

Having joined the Australian Labor Party (ALP) in 1954, Wran became a member of the State Executive in 1967. He also chaired the Labor Party's Legal and Constitutional Committee for a time. An atheist and free-thinker, Wran was sympathetic to many of the new human rights, social and environmental issues that were coming into prominence in the 1960s and 70s. He also had a deep-seated desire to improve the lives of ordinary working Australians. His speechwriter and friend Graham Freudenberg described it as "a Balmain version of *noblesse oblige*".[3]

In 1966, Wran took his first step towards active

involvement in politics when he sought Labor preselection for the NSW Legislative Council. It was a
peculiar institution. The Council had been reconstituted
in 1934 into a chamber of 60 members. The term was
12 years, with 15 MLCs retiring triennially. Upper house
members were elected by an electoral college consisting
of all members of both houses. The aim was to induce
into politics people like Wran who had expertise and
wanted to make a contribution to public life, but were
not prepared to take on the role of full-time politician.
In practice, the parties usually chose candidates on the
basis of loyalty rather than merit. The average age of
MLCs was high and the pace of activity often leisurely.
When the government controlled both houses, as it
did for most of the Coalition's term from 1965-76, the
Council was a rubber stamp rather than a house of
review.

Membership of the upper house was much sought after,
and it was a case of waiting in line. After several failed
attempts, Wran became an MLC on 12 March 1970. His
success was largely due to the support of the Leader
of the Opposition in the Council, Reg Downing.[4] A
legendary back-room figure in ALP politics, he became
an MLC in 1940 and was Leader of the Government
and a Minister from 1941-65. Downing had built
up a practice at the Bar to supplement his income in
Opposition but was still carrying much of the load in
the Council, having to lead on most bills. An astute
judge of character, Downing saw Wran's potential and
sponsored his rise. Wran became Deputy Leader of the

Opposition on 27 April 1971 and succeeded Downing on his retirement on 22 February 1972. Wran later commented that Downing was "head and shoulders above the rest. I learned a fair bit about politics from him".[5]

Wran's ability and Labor's inability to defeat Premier Bob Askin resulted in his rapid rise from the backwater of the Council to the summit of State politics.

Labor Leader

The Leader of the Opposition from 1968 was Patrick Darcy Hills. One of Labor's rising stars in the 1950s, he was nick-named the "Golden Boy". Hills had a successful term as Lord Mayor of Sydney from 1952-56, cleaning up the old, corrupt inner-city machine. He entered the Legislative Assembly in 1954 and five years later was promoted by Premier Joe Cahill, who was feeling the pressure of the job, to Minister Assisting the Premier, ranking fifth in cabinet seniority. By the 1970s, however, the gold had turned to grey. Hills had not adapted well to television, granted few interviews and made little attempt to use the media to generate favourable publicity. A conservative Catholic, he was uncomfortable with many of the new issues that Gough Whitlam had embraced as part of his revival of Federal Labor.

Bob Askin had won the 1965, 1968 and 1971 elections and Labor was becoming desperate to find a way out of the wilderness. To a growing number, Hills was a liability who had missed his chance. Among these was Party President and right-wing strong man John Ducker, who decided that, in spite of tribal loyalties, Hills had to go for the greater good.

Wran was the obvious replacement. He was a persuasive communicator, a credible alternative Premier, and had demonstrated his leadership potential in the Legislative Council. As a civil libertarian QC of progressive leanings, Wran had the appropriate image for the times – and he was a Balmain boy as well. Never deficient in ego and ambition, he embarked on the perilous pursuit of the ALP leadership.

Wran was not strongly associated with either the right or left factions. His industrial relations practice ensured he had support from important figures in the left, particularly Ray Gietzelt of the Miscellaneous Workers' Union. His friendship with key Labor lawyers such as Lionel Murphy and Jack Sweeney assisted him. Most importantly he won over the leader of the parliamentary left, Jack Ferguson.

Rodney Cavalier was a Labor MP 1978-88, a Minister 1984-88 and a friend and confidant of Ferguson. He has commented:

> Jack Ferguson had been in the Parliament since 1959, he had seen Wran around the place, saw the company he had kept and was not impressed. Jack Ferguson was a rock of integrity. He believed in what he believed. He could not take a false step. It was all very well for

Ducker and co to be advocating change because any sort of change had to be for the better, Jack required convincing that Wran was for the better.[6]

When Ferguson talked frankly and honestly with Wran he realised they had much in common:

Their values coincided though Neville was inclined to express his radicalism in sweeter terms. Jack respected that. The big difference was the education that had blessed Neville, the consequence of older, supportive siblings and parents who sacrificed much to enable the youngest to have the advantages denied to them. Jack had been the oldest in a family who were held together by a remarkable mother in the absence of a father who could not or would not hold down a job. Jack had left school at 12, he had been to war and worked very hard every day of his life up to and beyond his election to the NSW Parliament. Talks in earnest between Wran and Ferguson about shaking up Labor in NSW led to a trust that would be the bedrock of Wran's leadership. Doubt became respect, respect became absolute trust, friendship became an immense mutual affection that only Jack's death brought to an end.[7]

There were many impediments to a Wran leadership. He was in the wrong house and his resignation had to be engineered to ensure Labor did not lose his seat. A suitable Assembly electorate had to be found for him. Hills, who was not going to go quietly, had significant support from the caucus right, many of whom were suspicious of the high-flying Wran. An unlikely alliance of convenience between Ducker and Ferguson succeeded in executing the coup.

When Askin called an early election for 17 November 1973 the first part of the Wran assault commenced with his resignation from the Council. Hills fought back. Under ALP rules, Wran had to seek permission from the Party's Administrative Committee to resign his seat. The Opposition Leader vigorously opposed this, arguing that it would be seen as publicly undermining his position. In a humiliation for him and a portent of things to come, the motion to accept Wran's resignation was passed with only Hills dissenting.

Under the system of indirect election in use in the upper house, the ALP would lose Wran's position at a by-election unless a Liberal vacancy occurred as well, thus allowing proportional representation to come into effect. The difficulty was solved when the Whitlam Government appointed Liberal MLC Bernard Riley a Federal judge.

The ageing Member for the safe seat of Bass Hill, Clarrie Earl, was induced to retire. The ALP's Administrative Committee used the early election to justify the cancellation of a rank and file preselection ballot in his seat and installed Wran as candidate. He was elected with 60.69% of the primary vote, a swing of about 6 per cent against Labor.

Although Askin was re-elected in 1973, his victory was

not as decisive as many had expected. In a house of 99, the Government had 52 seats and Labor 44. Askin's recent record had inspired little enthusiasm among the voters. He lacked his previous drive and his government had lost momentum. However, they had been annoyed by Whitlam and a wave of disruptive strikes and had little faith in the alternative that Hills was offering. Askin was thus grudgingly given another term in office. With the appropriate leader, Labor had a reasonable chance of winning the next election.

The Parliamentary Labor Party assembled for the first time after the election on 3 December, with the party leadership the main item of business. The meeting had been preceded by intense lobbying by the Wran forces. Hills was more complacent. According to Cavalier:

> Wran and Ferguson had an arrangement whereby Jack would become the Deputy to Neville. Jack had expended every waking moment persuading doubters that Wran was the goods. More than once, he had to send a shattered Wran back into the fray. "Neville was dealing with boneheads as he visited members of caucus in their homes," Jack recalled. "He became terribly discouraged when some bonehead would tell him straight, he was not voting for him. That's what boneheads are like, I had to remind him. It was a good lesson for what was ahead." Notwithstanding Ferguson's labours, the machine was as equally committed to blocking Jack as they were to supporting Neville.[8]

The candidates were Wran, Hills and Kevin Stewart, a

former Hills supporter who believed his time had come. Wran received 18 votes, Hills 17, and Stewart nine. After distribution of preferences, Wran and Hills were tied on 22 votes each. Anticipating a close result, Ferguson had persuaded the returning officer, right-winger Vince Durick, that whoever was ahead on primaries should be the winner. He duly declared Wran elected. In spite of the opposition of ALP head office, Ferguson defeated Syd Einfeld for Deputy with one more vote than Wran.

Cavalier has reconstructed the voting figures as accurately as they will ever be.[9] The left and Ferguson acolytes delivered 14 votes for Wran. He had three right votes – Laurie Brereton, Terry Sheahan, Eric Bedford – plus his own. The four Stewart preferences were critical to Wran's victory. All were from the right, Peter Cox, Michael Maher, George Paciullo and Stewart himself:

> The right votes for Wran were not a product of machine pressure nor the beguilements of Ducker. Those three right primary votes (Brereton, Sheahan, Bedford) occurred because those three thought Neville Wran gave Labor a fighting chance of future victory, Hills none. The same calculations persuaded the four Stewart voters to give their preferences to Wran ... Neither Ducker nor the machine delivered a single vote to Wran. The thesis does not eliminate Ducker from considerable credit in the planning and altering the atmospherics that made the prospect of challenge legitimate.[10]

Wran was Labor Leader by the narrowest of margins.

The formidable challenges of consolidating his team, confronting the wily Askin, and winning the next election were before him.

Winning in 1976

Wran's shadow ministry was not, overall, a strong one. However, it had a formidable core. There were able and experienced veterans such Peter Cox (transport), Syd Einfeld (consumer affairs), Harry Jensen (local government) and Kevin Stewart (health). Don Day (primary industries), who had won the north coast seat of Casino in 1971, took the fight up to the Country Party. George Paciullo was a highly visible shadow sports spokesman. Two new, legally qualified MPs, Ron Mulock and Frank Walker, added depth. Wran appointed Mulock shadow attorney-general and justice minister. Walker had been defeated in the ballot for the shadow ministry after the 1973 election, a pay-back for his strong support of Wran and a blunt reminder that the right still had the numbers in caucus. According to Terry Sheahan, who was a Labor MP from 1973-88 and a Minister 1980-88, Walker became "a roving envoy for Wran and Jack Ferguson, and I have no doubt he was useful to Jack and to the new Whip, Pat Flaherty, in devising and implementing the Wran Opposition's parliamentary tactics from 1973-6. Frank was appointed Attorney-General and Leader of the House when we won in 1976".[11]

Wran was able to consolidate his authority because

he looked increasingly like a winner. Sheahan has commented:

> With his sheer talent, and infectious enthusiasm, [Wran] gradually garnered stoic support from many of those who filled leading roles in the shadow cabinet but had not supported him for the leadership. They could see how gifted he was, how hard he consistently worked – in the house, in the caucus and its committees, and 'around the traps' – and how successfully he was insulating State Labor from Federal Labor's woes. [12]

An important early Wran appointment was of Brian Dale as press secretary. Dale was covering state politics for the *Australian Financial Review* and he and Wran struck up a lasting friendship. He masterminded Wran's media strategy and became a key adviser in Government. Dale recalls of that time:

> The staff was small, conditions cramped, no mobile phones, no Twitter, Facebook or other devices. Contact with the electorate and voters (both supporters and potential) was direct. You went to see them or used the media to get messages across. Parliament was almost irrelevant to voters but was otherwise as the place to boost the confidence of our MPs, embarrass the Government and Ministers and imbue the Leader of the Opposition with confidence. The Legislative Assembly was important. In the old Parliament House, Wran and Ferguson shared a single suite of offices running along a long corridor up a stairway from the Parliament House foyer and along a narrow corridor from the equally cramped

parliamentary press gallery … By today's standards
it was primitive. Yet, it was, in the main, refreshingly
isolated from [ALP] head office. That meant a high
degree of independence for the leadership. Wran and
Ferguson, along with the then shadow ministers, knew
the party and the unions along with the platform,
the policy committees and the expectations. Branch
meetings, policy committees, their own activities, their
experiences, and their ALP commitment meant any
policy announced had reference to the platform and
not outside interest and lobbyists.[13]

Under the supervision of Labor State Secretary, Peter
Westerway, the platform had been extensively revised
and updated in the early 1970s. The Opposition went
into the 1976 campaign with "real policies, policies
developed and refined, policies that would resonate".[14]

Effective media management was one of Wran's great
strengths, but there was more to it than spin, as Dale
has noted:

The basis of the Wran approach was that we had to
have a story to tell. That was how we did it then. No
bland, say nothing, media releases. No glib responses
or one-liners, no zingers. If a question was asked,
then it was answered in normal conversation, not just
a series of the same words in different arrangements.
Sure, Wran went through issues and possible questions
before any media event, but he never went in with
a series of quotes to be repeated *ad nauseam* until
everyone's eyes glazed over. He would make notes in
his ever-present spiral notebook, recoding a single or

a couple of words to rejig his thoughts. That was how he'd done it at the Bar. Wran had an innate sense of what made a story. He could phrase his responses to fit the story and ensure his words were reported. In keeping with his dictum to avoid negative criticism of everything, he always injected a positive note in all the media events.[15]

Askin stepped down as Premier in January 1975. In his final years in parliament he seemed detached and uninterested. However, he was still capable of delivering a devastating counterpunch to any Opposition Member who provoked him. Deputy Leader Eric Willis took over most of the business in the Assembly. To the surprise of many, Askin was succeeded not by his Deputy but Lands Minister Tom Lewis. Against Askin and Willis, Wran began to make some headway but it was hard going. When Lewis took over, Wran soon became dominant in the chamber.

Ron Mulock was an MP 1971-88, a Minister 1976-88 and Deputy Premier 1984-88. He described Lewis as "an example of the 'Peter principle': he was adequate where he was, but he could not deliver when he moved up to the top job. I do not think he was prepared to do the necessary hard work nor was he too quick on the uptake".[16] Mulock added:

We were confident that Neville Wran would quickly show his ascendancy over Lewis and this proved to be so. Neville had really hit his straps and was making a very favourable impression in parliament and with the public. He was a skilful performer in debate on the

> floor of the house and also very accomplished in the
> media, especially television. He had a bit of a thespian
> approach, but it was not overdone. It was just right.[17]

In January 1976, Willis took his revenge and overthrew Lewis in a surprise coup. Many Liberal MPs had become convinced that they were heading for electoral disaster under Lewis. The incoming Premier faced a difficult by-election in the Coalition seat of Monaro and had been warned that the Liberal Federal Government was planning a tough budget later in the year. He was also under pressure to go to the polls before voters forgot the Whitlam Government which had been resoundingly defeated in November 1975. Willis decided to call an early election for 1 May.

The *Sydney Morning Herald*'s State political correspondent John O'Hara, no friend of Labor, in a perceptive profile at the beginning of the campaign commented that Wran projected "a balanced blend of cultivated urbanity and earthiness".[18] O'Hara noted a dualism in him: "ardent reformer and man of expedience". Since becoming Opposition Leader, Wran had been "a one man parade of arresting political ideas and initiatives" who had set "a cracking pace in selling himself to the public and taking the attack to the Government".[19] In the Assembly, Wran was notable for "nimbleness in debate and his at times brilliant rhetoric. But his strongest asset has been his instinct for dealing with radio and television outside parliament".[20]

Wran campaigned effectively, using the slogan "Let's put

this State in better shape". He told the voters that the only legacy of the Coalition's rule was high prices and poor services. The railways, in particular, were a financial and political liability. Shadow transport minister Peter Cox highlighted inadequate rolling stock, unreliable services and old and unsafe carriages. Under the Coalition NSW had fallen behind the other states. Labor had the policies and dynamism to put it back on top and restore to its citizens the quality of life they deserved. Wran attempted to defuse the predictable charge of "Where's the money coming from?" by saying that Labor would fund its program through the sale of surplus government land and eliminating waste and inefficiencies. He worked hard to ensure there was a clear distinction between State and Federal issues, making it plain that Whitlam was not welcome in the campaign.

As well as the "bread and butter" issues, Wran also had an awareness of broader horizons. The environment, anti-discrimination and the equality of all before the law were mentioned in his policy speech. In an interview during the campaign, he held up South Australia, where Don Dunstan was re-inventing ideas of what State government was about, as a model for what he would like to see happen in NSW. Wran specifically mentioned creating a film industry, more support for those with disabilities, and homosexual law reform.[21]

Willis ran a negative campaign, portraying the Opposition as inexperienced, irresponsible, socialist and under the control of the unions. Wran's extravagant promises would bankrupt the State. Labor in government in NSW would be as disastrous as Whitlam had been in Canberra. The voters would be wise to stick with a government that had proven its competence.

In return, Wran effectively launched a scare campaign of his own. Willis had written to Prime Minister Malcolm Fraser endorsing his proposal to allow the States to re-enter the income tax field. Dale remembers that Wran's office received leaked copies of the letter "from about four anonymous sources in the Canberra bureaucracy and it was reproduced in an advertisement along with an extract from an *Australian Financial Review* editorial attacking the idea of the States getting into income tax"[22]. Wran claimed that what was already a high-taxing government would now go even further and impose "double taxation". Under Labor, there would be no NSW income tax.

The results were in doubt for some time. After a painfully slow count, the ALP narrowly won Gosford, Hurstville and Monaro from the Liberals and Blue Mountains from a pro-Liberal Independent. Labor easily took Ashfield where the long-time Liberal MP had retired. Wran was finally able to claim victory with 50 of the 99 seats. In terms of votes, the result was more clear cut. The ALP polled 49.75 per cent of the primary vote compared to the Coalition's 46.32 per cent, a swing of 6.83 per cent. Askin's serial redistributions had biased the electoral system against Labor.

The 1976 election was a hinge between old and new

politics in NSW. Although perennial issues such as public transport were crucial, Wran's superior media skills, "with it" image, and awareness of new currents in society had given him a narrow victory.

Consolidating: 1976-1978

The fifty Labor members of the Legislative Assembly gathered to elect the new ministry on 13 May 1976. Wran and Ferguson were re-elected unopposed as Leader and Deputy. Paul Landa, a Labor lawyer and Wran adherent, narrowly defeated the incumbent Leader in the Legislative Council, Lee Serisier. Peter Cox topped the poll with 46 votes and Harry Jensen and Ron Mulock each received 43. Frank Walker was successful this time. In a slap in the face for the old guard, Walker ranked fifth and Landa sixth in seniority in a cabinet of 18.[23]

Although Wran did not have the numbers in cabinet, Mulock (who successively held the portfolios of Justice and Services, Mineral Resources, Education, Health, Transport and Attorney-General) commented that he had plenty of support:

> I had told him way back in 1973 when he was running
> for Leader of the Opposition that, even though I
> wasn't voting for him, if he was elected he would have
> my support - and he did. Of course, I reserved the
> right to state my views and to disagree on issues when
> I felt it appropriate. There were a lot of other people
> in cabinet who recognised that he was the leader, that

he had won the election for us, and with that came a position of personal power. There were a number of Catholics including myself taking that attitude. I know that there wasn't any organised opposition from that quarter to Neville Wran in the whole of the time he was Premier.[24]

Wran often used cabinet's Policy and Priorities Committee as an inner cabinet and whole of government co-ordinating mechanism. It consisted of the six top ranking Ministers: Jack Ferguson (Public Works and Ports), Jack Renshaw (Treasurer), Peter Cox (Transport), Pat Hills (Mines and Energy), Frank Walker (Attorney-General), and Paul Landa (Industrial Relations). Wran had a majority with the support of Ferguson, Walker and Landa.

Wran continued to rely on Ferguson to manage caucus and ALP head office to manage the party. Mulock has astutely observed:

I don't think in the whole of the period that Neville Wran was in the Legislative Assembly as Leader that he controlled actual votes. Other people controlled them for him to the degree that they were able to. In essence, the people that did it for Neville were Jack Ferguson from the left and head office - the same combination that delivered for Neville in the 1973 leadership ballot against Pat Hills. By and large, they also delivered in government.[25]

Wran appointed a member of the Public Service Board, Gerry Gleeson, as head of the Premier's Department on

Ferguson's recommendation. Wran relied on Gleeson to control the public service and make sure it ran efficiently. He was a source of information for Wran on his ministers and occasionally a bureaucratic hitman. It was an inspired appointment as Gleeson was ruthlessly efficient and completely loyal to the Premier. Under Gleeson the locus of public service power switched from the Public Service Board to the Premier's Department.

In his own office, Wran created the Ministerial Advisory Unit (MAU) to provide him with independent advice and analysis. It was an exceptionally talented group: David Hill, Nigel Stokes, Milton Cockburn and Tom Fitzgerald. Cockburn has said that the MAU's role was basically economic:

> If it had a *raison d'etre* it was to reconcile Labor's policy commitments with Wran's determination not to let public spending get out of control which would have led to state tax increases. The Whitlam Government was always a warning to him. Wran had campaigned effectively (and misleadingly) on the grounds of no state income tax. He was adamant that he did not want to be saddled with a reputation for new taxes or tax increases so the MAU's major focus was always on budget control and economic development issues. Despite occasional fights, Treasury head Norm Oakes came to see the MAU as an ally.[26]

The Premier would sometimes ask the MAU to trouble-shoot when the Government ran into problems:

> For example, when Wran came under criticism from

within the party for not repealing the *Summary Offences Act*, as promised, he said to me one day, in effect: find out why we haven't done this and get it done. It turned out that Frank Walker and his department had got bogged down in bureaucratic and ministerial opposition. We were able to shepherd it through, help sort out the more targeted legislation (such as the *Offences in Public Places Act*) that would replace the old blunderbuss act and give the whole reform Wran's *imprimatur*. Frank was very happy for us to get involved because he saw it as a way out of the log jam. But that was never really the role envisioned for it. As Gerry Gleeson beefed up the Premiers' Department, transforming it into a policy development unit, it gradually took on this sort of role.[27]

The MAU also had a political function:

It was the contact point for candidates and members in marginal seats. Candidates, in particular, could contact us for assistance in running their campaigns, such as sorting out money for local projects in the electorates. Sometimes we could, sometimes we couldn't. We worked closely with one of Treasurer Ken Booth's staffers to provide money from the old Sport and Recreation Fund (a large amount of the money from the Soccer Pools was hypothecated into the fund administered by the Minister for Sport). Ken was always careful to look after certain Opposition MPs too, which is why he never got into Bridget McKenzie/Ros Kelly type problems. Peter Anderson, Rodney Cavalier, Michael Egan, Bill McCarthy and other marginal seat backbenchers were all active in using the MAU as a contact point for Wran's attention.[28]

After appointing a Speaker, the Wran Government's numbers on the floor of the Legislative Assembly dropped to 49. The Opposition had 48 MPs and there was one Independent, John Hatton (South Coast). Hatton was, at this stage, sympathetic to Labor and often, though not invariably, voted with the Government. Absenteeism among Opposition members also sometimes allowed it to win votes comfortably. On the whole, Wran's small majority caused him few problems.

Wran's powerful performances in the Legislative Assembly strengthened the Government's position. He alternated effortlessly between the fluent, logical argument of the QC and outbursts of savage vituperation. The Opposition benches were often noticeably silent when Wran was in full flight, with Coalition MPs afraid of calling down his wrath on them. Rodney Cavalier recalls that on one occasion in question time Wran became

> ... irritated beyond endurance by the constant interjections of a backbencher from the Nats. Neville stopped mid-answer. He was a master of the studied pause, a prolonged silence, permitting the noisome to flay against the rock of his calm: 'Can I say this, Mr Speaker, if the member continues to interject then I will be forced to acquaint this house with his behaviour in the past fortnight, behaviour that, even by his standards, is particularly wicked'. The member fell silent and changed colour. Afterwards I asked Neville what he had on him: 'Nothing. Nothing at all

but it's a safe bet with a bastard like that he has done
something wicked in any given fortnight'.[29]

Wran convincingly demonstrated his superiority over a series of Liberal leaders. His mastery of the house rallied his team and demoralised the Opposition. It contributed significantly to his electoral success.

Although he had an iconoclastic streak, Wran also respected fundamental institutions such as the courts and parliament. During his time as premier, a number of improvements were made to the way the Legislative Assembly functioned. The use of committees went through a major revival. The work of the Pecuniary Interest and Public Funding Committees was of major importance in the establishment of legislative schemes in both these areas. A report by the Joint Standing Committee on Road Safety led to the introduction of random breath testing. The Public Accounts Committee was revived, and its powers strengthened. A series of important reforms enhanced parliamentary scrutiny of public expenditure. Useful improvements were made to the Standing Orders.

A major achievement in Wran's first term was reform of the Legislative Council. By the 1970s, such a body was widely seen as anachronistic and undemocratic. The Premier's attitude to the Council was not improved by the fact that the Opposition-controlled upper house soon began to amend the Wran Government's legislation. There were 74 successful non-government amendments to bills in the 1976-78 session, compared to none in 1975-76. A major piece of Labor legislation, the Anti-Discrimination Bill, was heavily amended against the Government's will.

In June 1977, Wran unveiled his proposal for a popularly elected Council. It would be elected on a State-wide basis using proportional representation. Voting would be for lists of party candidates rather than being preferential. The Government's announced timetable was for a referendum in mid-1978 with the first election later in the year. Labor had a reasonable chance of winning enough seats to give it control of the Legislative Council. This was a disturbing prospect for the Opposition. Under the current electoral legislation, a redistribution could not be held until after the next general election. If Labor gained control of the Council it could change this and bring in new boundaries redressing the Askin bias. To avoid this, the Opposition did a deal with Wran. In return for a guarantee that the first Council election would be held with the next Assembly election and the dropping of the list system in favour of optional preferential voting, the Coalition agreed to support the upper house reform referendum.

Malcolm Turnbull, then a journalist for *The Bulletin*, wrote a feature article claiming that the Opposition had out-manoeuvred Wran.[30] In fact, the Premier had come to the conclusion that the holding of a referendum, Legislative Council election and general election within 12 months was not politically or logistically feasible. His supposed concession on the timing of the first Council poll was sheer bluff. The compromise gave Wran all he needed plus the image of a statesman-like reformer allowing the people a voice in the election of the upper house. The referendum was carried overwhelmingly with 85 per cent voting in favour.[31]

Wran quickly imposed his stamp on the government. Influenced by the political disasters of the Whitlam era, he insisted on steadiness, internal unity, and a moderate, gradualist approach to governing. Wran's style was pragmatic, flexible and cautious. As he expressed it: "Some Labor governments in the past rushed in and tried to do everything at once, we tried to keep pace with community opinion. When the community didn't have an opinion we'd endeavour to create an environment whereby the community would accept it as if they'd thought of it themselves".[32]

According to one academic commentator:

> Much to the surprise of many, the first six months of Wran Labor Government treated us to virtual blunder-free government for the first time in many years. The Premier's self-confidence never wavered in public, and his political judgment was almost faultless. Labor's ministers slipped almost unobtrusively into a pattern of calm management as if born to the job and appeared to be working hard to come to grips with implementing some of Labor's promised reforms.[33]

Wran was an economic traditionalist who favoured responsible public expenditure, creating jobs and facilitating development. His message was that investment in NSW was always welcome. This approach and his political moderation ensured relations with the business community were generally positive. Business was not inclined to back an obvious loser like the NSW Liberal Party.

Rural NSW was not neglected by Wran – partly because he believed there were seats to be won, partly because he saw it as part of his job to advance the interests of country as well as city areas. By May 1983, 17 rural cabinet meetings had been held throughout the state. They were usually followed by the announcement of some largesse for the local area. Asked after one of these expeditions if the Government expected to gain support as a result, Wran smiled and replied: "We are not here to lose votes".[34] At the 1981 election, Labor won seven of 23 country seats: Albury, Bathurst, Burrinjuck, Clarence, Monaro, Northern Tablelands and Murrumbidgee.[35]

Media relations were overseen by Brian Dale (assisted by Peter Barron who succeeded him in 1981) with much adroitness. The centralisation of contact with the media and Wran's masterly performances meant that the Premier became the undoubted star of the Government.

Wran was very conscious that his Government was on trial and had to prove its worth if it was to be re-elected. He spent much time connecting with the voters personally. Dale remembers those days well:

> When Parliament wasn't sitting, Wran and I were on the road seeing community groups, local ALP branches, union gatherings, events and anything we could dream

up to get his presence out there. No street meetings though. Over the period in Opposition and the first years of Government there were very few places throughout the State that Wran and I hadn't visited. From Louth and Pooncarrie, almost at opposite ends of the Darling River, Macquarie Marshes and Menindee Lakes (with great yabbies), northern rainforests and the open Western District, the Monaro and the Murray, Bourke and Brewarrina, many others. If there was a vote, a TV or radio station, a local newspaper we were sure to visit. Wran was present at ALP meetings, schools and hospitals, with me a few steps behind. No advance teams, no multiple staff, mostly no car and driver and a bumpy flight home on a small plane to a diminishing personal life.[36]

Moderate politics did not preclude reform, rather it was a platform for it. A number of election commitments were quickly delivered on. Public transport fares were cut by 20 per cent, local government rate rises were pegged at 12 per cent, and a Prices Commission was established (although it achieved little in the long term). The Land Commission (Landcom), established at the same time, delivered blocks of land to first home buyers at affordable prices. Dairy farmers outside the Sydney milk zone were given access to this lucrative market, something the Country Party in office had denied them.

Other reforms followed. The *Anti-Discrimination Act* was passed, the Ethnic Affairs Commission set up, and a Women's Advisory Council and Women's Co-ordination

Unit in the Premier's Department established. The law was amended to remove the stigma of illegitimacy. The scope of the *Consumer Protection Act* was enlarged and a separate Department of Consumer Affairs created. Date-stamping of food was introduced and tenants were protected by the establishment of the Rental Bond Board. The *Heritage Act* was passed.

Eric Willis never adjusted to Opposition and his poor performance led to his replacement by Peter Coleman in December 1977. Coleman was a barrister, author and intellectual, but not much of a politician. He had a dour, aloof public persona and Wran soon had his measure.

Willis resigned from Parliament, causing a by-election in his marginal seat of Earlwood on 15 July 1978. The ALP had an attractive candidate in young solicitor Ken Gabb; the Liberals fielded Alan Jones, later the king of Sydney talkback radio. Wran and Labor put enormous effort into the campaign and were amply rewarded: Gabb won the seat with a swing of over 8 per cent.

Wran called an early election for 7 October 1978. He had a record of promises delivered, solid achievement, stability in government, and had created an appealing, dependable public image. Unemployment was down and the economy was healthy. Capital works spending had been boosted but taxes had not been increased. The Government's slogan was "Wran's our man".

The Opposition struggled to find a credible line of attack, finally claiming that the Government was about to unleash a wave of socialism and permissiveness on

NSW. Unsurprisingly, the voters were not convinced. The result was a stunning victory for Wran. Labor won 63 of the 99 Assembly seats, with a primary vote of 57.77 per cent, a swing of 8.02 per cent. Opposition Leader Coleman lost his seat. Labor also won control of the Legislative Council, which it retained until it lost office in 1988.

Peaking: 1978-81

Wran's commanding victory in the 1978 poll strengthened his authority in cabinet and caucus. It did not, however, transform him into an egotistical autocrat, a temptation many lesser leaders would have succumbed to. Milton Cockburn, who served in Wran's Ministerial Advisory Unit, has said:

> Wran was a genuinely consultative Premier in regard to his staff. His first meeting every morning was with Brian Dale and Peter Barron and they'd often spend an hour going through the political and media issues of the day. Wran would often appear in your doorway seeking information or advice and he would frequently come around personally. From time to time he would also hold pizza and beer dinners in one of the rooms in the State Office Block and the staff (Brian Dale, Peter Barron, Graham Freudenberg, Ministerial Advisory Unit, Private Secretary Denise Darlow) were all encouraged to speak freely, criticise decisions taken or not taken, and give ideas. Wran was always happy to take things on board.[37]

It is a tribute to Wran that, in spite of the tantrums they occasionally endured, most of his core staff became life-long friends.

Ron Mulock has commented:

> For the whole of the period that I was in the Wran and Unsworth cabinets the main way in which a decision was taken was by consensus. When that is the method, if people hold back and don't state an opinion it's their responsibility. The whole system would fall apart if everybody remained silent and didn't express their real views about a particular issue outside their own portfolio. You made your own decision as to whether you were going to contribute to the debate. Only on a very small number of major matters was a vote taken. Personally, Neville varied between being quite amenable and at other times a bully, but nobody got gagged.[38]

The Premier used his political strength after the 1978 "Wranslide" to implement major constitutional reforms. Changes to electoral system in 1979 provided for optional preferential voting and abolished the weighting of rural electorates, with the maximum permitted variation from quota for all seats being fixed at 10 per cent. These changes were entrenched in the *Constitution Act* so that they could not be repealed without a referendum. A four year term for the Legislative Assembly and compulsory disclosure of Members' pecuniary interests were approved by referenda held simultaneously with the 1981 election. Legislation providing for public funding of elections and disclosure of political donations was passed and came into force in 1981.

The Wran Government delivered significant reforms in other areas. The *Environmental Planning and Assessment Act*, *Land and Environment Court Act* and *Coastal Protection Act* were passed in 1979, and the *Historic Houses Act* the following year. The *Summary Offences Act*, which Askin had controversially used against anti-Vietnam war activists and other protesters, was repealed, and replaced with a series of Acts decriminalising "victimless crimes". The scope of the *Anti-Discrimination Act* was widened, and equal opportunity programs instituted throughout the public sector. The Legal Services Commission was created in 1979 to improve the provision of legal aid. Sexual assault laws were reformed in 1981. The recommendations of the Nagle Royal Commission into the Department of Corrective Services were adopted as a blueprint for prison reform. A Corrective Services Commission was established under reformer Tony Vinson. However, he resigned in frustration after two years.

Wran's second term was not without difficulties. A personal one was that in 1980 he had surgery for prostate cancer. Graham Freudenberg has described the unexpected consequences:

> Next day, he awoke in St Vincent's Hospital after his operation to find himself without a voice. Further examination revealed a throat tumour, possibly cancer. The unsuspected growth was found to be

43

non-malignant but scarcely benign: its pressure over the years had badly damaged the vocal chord. The outcome of a delicate operation and innovative post-operative treatment remained in doubt for a month. Wran retained a voice, its distinctive rasp the delight of mimics and Wran storytellers, but for those who could remember, a painful contrast with his strong clear voice before June 1980.[39]

In 1979, that carnivorous beast, the NSW right, decided to increase its control over the Government and the parliamentary party. This was to be achieved by admitting Legislative Council Members, who had a separate party room, to caucus. In 1977, the right had changed party rules so that MLCs were no longer selected by proportional representation. After that, head office controlled all upper house pre-selections, producing a tightly regimented group of foot soldiers. The effect of admitting them to caucus would be to add a bloc of right wingers who would vote as directed by the machine.

This was completely unacceptable to Ferguson and the left and, initially, to Wran, who made no secret of his contempt for the MLCs. However, ALP President John Ducker vehemently and humiliatingly reminded the Premier of his dependence on head office. Wran was forced into a situation where he had no good option, just a bad and worse one. He had to choose between his two main supporters in the party, a conflict he had fervently sought to avoid. Finally, he buckled to the big battalions and sided with the ruthless Ducker rather than the more congenial Ferguson, who was understandably furious. The Premier threw all his guile and energy into trying to find a way out.

A rancorous split in the Labor Party and Government developed. In May 1979, caucus accepted a compromise promoted by Wran: that MLCs only be admitted after the 1984 election when they would all be directly elected. Remorseless pressure was applied by head office and the motion was carried by 34 votes to 26.

There were bitter confrontations at the June 1979 Annual Conference over the rule change. The right was victorious, but was forced to make a further concession: Labor MLCs would be required to become full-time parliamentarians. As many were union officials, they would have to choose between that and their upper house seats. When all MLCs were full-time, they would be admitted to the caucus. After anger had cooled, Wran and Ferguson patched up their relationship and it was soon stronger than ever.

Factional disputation again damaged the Wran Government's image in July 1980 when Labor MLC Peter Baldwin was viciously beaten in his home. He was one of a group of young left activists challenging the right's control of the ALP in inner Sydney. The identity of his assailant has never been discovered but the assault was undoubtedly motivated by Baldwin's political activities. The bashing and subsequent investigations put the spotlight on corruption and criminality in inner city Labor branches.

In June 1981, there were widespread power blackouts in Sydney, the Hunter, and the Illawarra. Major problems in the electricity system were soon revealed. Wran took personal control and accepted full responsibility. Instead of making excuses, he admitted that things had not been well handled and said that the public's "justifiable anger" had "registered loud and clear".[40]

> There is no point beating around the bush. There is a crisis. All this equipment has broken down at the same time. We are sorry for the inconvenience. We are sorry there is a bit of a mess, but it is not going to kill anyone if we all act sensibly. If we turn off the odd light here and there we will be back to normal in a week or so.[41]

Emergency measures were instituted, and the system managed to get through the winter months without further serious problems. Wran's projection of bluff honesty and coolness in a crisis was perfectly calculated to deflect voter anger and reinforce his image as a "safe pair of hands".

If a government is, on the whole, performing well and the voters have confidence in it, they are inclined to forgive its occasional transgressions, particularly if they have no faith in the alternative. Both of these factors came into play in the 1981 election.

The Opposition produced a series of disastrous leaders. Peter Coleman was succeeded by John Mason, who was so incompetent that he was not even given the chance to lose an election. On 1 June 1981, he was deposed by his Deputy, Bruce McDonald, whose aggressive performances in the Assembly had impressed his colleagues. McDonald was the fifth Liberal Leader since the retirement of Askin in January 1975. His reputation was soon damaged by the exposure of dubious business dealings. A brash blusterer, McDonald failed to inspire any confidence among the voters, particularly compared to Wran.

Labor's strategy for the election to be held on 19 September 1981 again focussed on the Premier. The theme was "It's got to be Wran". In his policy speech, he made much of the revival of the economy under Labor. NSW now had the lowest unemployment rate in Australia. The economy was growing strongly in every sector and region. It was planned and balanced growth which protected the environment. Taxes had not been increased in five successive Budgets and services had been maintained at a high level.

Wran took advantage of the waning popularity of Liberal Prime Minister Fraser to warn that the only thing that could jeopardise the State's prosperity was the policies of the Federal Government, policies he had vigorously resisted but which the NSW Opposition supported. The watchwords of Labor in office were "reform, progress and equality". Wran sought a mandate for a further three years of "strong, stable, vigorous, united government".[42]

The Opposition claimed Wran had substituted image politics for achievement. McDonald offered, instead, "real priorities" which put "the people's interests ahead of those of government, big unions, big spending and big images. I am saying to you that slogans and jingles are merely the trenches in which the Labor Government seeks to hide from reality".[43] It was a misguided and ineffective strategy. Most voters liked the image and realised there was substance behind it.

The result was an overwhelming vote of confidence in the Wran Government, which was re-elected with six more seats. Labor won 69, the Liberals and National Country Party 14 each. The Government's primary vote was down 2.04 per cent to 55.73 per cent, but a fairer redistribution translated into more electorates. John Hatton was returned in South Coast. The Opposition Leader again lost his seat, with Independent Ted Mack defeating McDonald in North Shore.

Nemesis: 1981-86

After the 1981 election, National Country Party Leader Leon Punch made a bid for the Opposition leadership as both the Liberals and National Country Party each had 14 Assembly seats. To have as the alternative premier in Australia's most urbanised state the leader of a rump rural party would have been a gift beyond imagining for Wran. After much unseemly wrangling, Liberal John Dowd eventually became Leader of the Opposition, but relations between the Opposition parties remained strained and no coalition agreement was able to be negotiated.

A long-term goal of Wran's was to renew his ministry with able young backbenchers. This had the additional benefit of strengthening his position in cabinet as the new recruits knew only the Wran era and were loyal to him, although not unthinkingly so. It was initially a slow process, but gained speed as Wran's power and prestige increased. Jack Hallam became Deputy Leader in the Legislative Council and a minister in 1978 and Terry Sheahan joined Cabinet in 1980. Both were from the right. Peter Anderson, Laurie Brereton, Mike Cleary and Paul Whelan, also from the right, were elected after the 1981 poll, and Bob Carr in 1986. From the left, Rodney Cavalier and Bob Debus became ministers in 1984, and Ken Gabb in 1986. From 1981 onwards, Wran had the numbers in a talented cabinet.

Wran's political predominance sparked much speculation that he would move to Canberra, take over from incumbent Bill Hayden, and win the prime ministership. His appointment as ALP Federal President in 1980 did nothing to quell the rumours. Ron Mulock observed: "It was usually Neville who started the rumours about moving to Canberra. He would throw it out to liven things up in the media and stir up those interested in the succession. Maybe he wanted to be mischievous or perhaps he was just plain bored".[44] Mulock believed that "Neville's great desire was to go Federal, but he was thwarted by the course of political events".[45] Bob Hawke entered the Commonwealth Parliament and the NSW right decided to back him. Hawke became Labor Leader in February 1983 and Prime Minister the following month.

Many governments by their third term have lost their early zeal and are content to coast. Wran continued to deliver. Hospital beds were relocated from the inner-city to growth areas in Sydney's west in the face of fierce resistance from vested interests in the medical profession and union movement. In October 1982, after an intense, eight hour meeting, Cabinet agreed to preserve 90,000 hectares of northern rainforest. The pioneering *Aboriginal Land Rights Act* was passed in 1983. The *Mental Health Act 1983*, based on David Richmond's report, revolutionised the treatment of the mentally ill. One of its main recommendations was deinstitutionalisation of patients. While the intention was positive, subsequent lack of adequate funding undermined implementation of the reforms.

The *Community Welfare Act* was revised and updated in 1983. The Housing Commission, which had become an inflexible fiefdom, was abolished and replaced by a Department with a brief to introduce an integrated housing policy. Legislation in 1983 provided for the establishment and operation of community justice centres. The *Anti-Discrimination Act* was amended so that (with certain exemptions) it included discrimination on the basis of intellectual disability. Male homosexuality ceased to be a criminal offence as a result of a private member's bill sponsored by Wran in May 1984.

In the early 1980s, Wran was at the summit of his achievement. After that, barely anything went right for him.

On 15 March 1983, Nick Greiner replaced the

uninspiring Dowd as Leader of the Opposition.[46] Greiner was not in the typical Liberal party mould. He was born in Budapest on 23 April 1947 of a Catholic father and Jewish mother. The family came to Australia in 1951 and was a classic migrant success story. Entering the Legislative Assembly at a by-election in 1980, Greiner quickly showed ability in the house and gained credibility with the media. He had intellectual substance, with an impressive background in academic economics at Sydney University and a Harvard MBA and was a polished performer in public. Greiner repaired coalition relations and a joint shadow cabinet was formed for the first time since 1976. With the assistance of his senior policy adviser Gary Sturgess, Greiner began to develop comprehensive policies for government.

The Liberals now had a leader who was an electorally appealing option as premier. Greiner challenged Wran's supremacy and exploited the Government's difficulties to the maximum. Sturgess has commented: "It is significant that Greiner was utterly unafraid of Wran. I was impressed by the fact that he would take it on the chin and go back again. That was extraordinarily important given the significance of the corruption issue as a way of besting Wran in the chamber".[47]

The economy became a major problem for the Wran Government during its third term.[48] Wran had delivered on his promise to give the public transport system a much-needed injection of capital funding. Expenditure on major public works projects had assisted economic revival and solid employment growth. Taxes were not increased in the first five Budgets. This was partly a result of some creative financial management, with the generous financial reserves of major statutory authorities being scooped out. By the early 1980s, this was no longer viable as the reserves had been reduced to dangerously low levels. At the same time, a severe global recession affected Australia, with NSW hard hit. The State's economy was damaged by a prolonged drought. The Fraser Government made serious reductions in Commonwealth grants to NSW. More capital funding had to be found to deal with electricity supply problems. A grand plan championed by Wran for major expansion of the aluminium industry in the Hunter region collapsed due to the international recession. The coal and steel industries experienced a significant downturn. As revenue declined, the Government was forced to raise taxes and charges sharply and increase the deficit.

Relations with the trade union movement deteriorated as the Wran Government had less largesse to placate its allies at the Labor Council. It was forced to make spending cuts, such as a freeze on public sector employment, and demand greater efficiencies, particularly in that lumbering behemoth, the State Rail Authority. Attempts by Transport Minister Peter Cox and the head of State Rail, David Hill, to make such basic reforms as eliminating firemen on electric and diesel locomotives and no-longer employing carpenters to maintain aluminium carriages led to prolonged strikes which greatly inconvenienced the travelling public.

Most seriously of all, Wran came under sustained assault over corruption in the police and justice system. There was no shortage of material: prostitution, casinos and the drug trade were flourishing with the protection of corrupt police, who were in turn protected by friends higher up the ladder.[49] The Opposition had finally found a line of attack that paid off, running with scandal after scandal, some dubious, some not, and by inference linking Wran personally with the sensational revelations.

When confronted with evidence of widespread corruption, Wran made the serious error of trying to obfuscate and cover-up. Rather than admitting that there was a real problem that needed to be urgently addressed, he over-confidently assumed his political and parliamentary skills would enable him to defuse the issue. He would have been better advised to examine seriously the many credible allegations that emerged.

Deputy Police Commissioner Bill Allen, whose rapid rise through the ranks had been due to Wran's personal intervention, was found guilty of serious misconduct. He was demoted and allowed to resign in April 1982. Corrective Services Minister Rex Jackson was forced to resign in October 1983 over allegations he had accepted bribes to release prisoners from gaol early. Jackson was subsequently charged, convicted and imprisoned. In February 1984, the Melbourne *Age* newspaper published details of unauthorised telephone surveillance carried out by NSW police. The tapes contained sensational revelations about organised crime, drug trafficking, and corruption involving police, the judiciary and politicians.

Just six weeks after Greiner became Opposition Leader, the corruption issue dramatically ensnared Wran. The ABC's *Four Corners* program claimed that he had used Chief Magistrate Murray Farquhar as an intermediary to have fraud charges against the head of the NSW Rugby League, Kevin Humphreys, dismissed.[50]

Attorney-General Paul Landa assumed Wran was guilty and saw this as his opportunity to become Premier. He urged Wran to establish a Royal Commission under Chief Justice Sir Laurence Street to investigate the *Four Corners* claims. In doing so, Landa disregarded legal advice which provided other options for handling the situation. The bumptious Landa's high opinion of his leadership (and legal) ability was not shared by many of his colleagues. Wran agreed to the Royal Commission and decided to step aside during its course, but cabinet and caucus only found out when the Attorney made the public announcement, enhancing resentment of Landa. Wran was disappointed with his protégé's lack of support, made obvious in Landa's statement, where any expression of confidence in the Premier's innocence was noticeably lacking. However, Wran tolerated Landa's political gamble and explained it away by saying that "you had to take chances to get ahead in politics" and Landa was a "main chancer".[51]

Wran stood aside as Premier on 10 May 1983. Ron Mulock described his reaction as:

> ... a mixture of anger, frustration and resignation.

> He accepted that standing down was the right course
> of action and he believed he would be vindicated.
> It certainly came as a shock to the cabinet but on
> reflection we all agreed it was the wisest course. Jack
> Ferguson would be Acting Premier. The effect on the
> Government was minimal. It was business as usual
> under Jack's leadership.[52]

Although Wran was completely exonerated by Street's report, it was a scorching experience for him. According to Mulock, the Royal Commission "had a long term affect upon his psyche. It really caused him to think a lot about whether the game was worth it".[53]

Belatedly, Wran tried to counter the damage caused by the corruption issue with reforms to the police. He increased the powers of the Ombudsman to investigate complaints against police and upgraded the Internal Affairs Branch. Most significantly, in 1983, in the face of determined resistance, a civilian Police Board was given overall control of the force as recommended by the 1981 Lusher Report into police administration.[54] Implementation of other recommendations by Lusher did, to some extent, improve police culture. Ultimately, however, these measures did not succeed in combatting entrenched, systemic corruption.

In 1984, Wran set up Special Commissions of Inquiry under Justice RF Cross into corruption allegations made by Ian Sinclair, Deputy Leader of the Federal National Party, and investigative journalist Bob Bottom. Both sets of claims were found to be baseless.[55] Wran took advantage of the temporary respite this gave him and called an early election for 24 March 1984.

In view of the economic difficulties NSW had been through, Wran concentrated on talking up the future. He told the voters that Labor's sound financial management, particularly in recent hard times, had provided the basis for a period of renewed growth and falling unemployment. There were good times ahead for the people of NSW. The Government's responsible handling of the economy now allowed it to deliver further benefits. Wran outlined a series of concessions on electricity charges, motor vehicle insurance and registration, and land and payroll tax. A particularly attractive piece of electoral bait (never delivered on) was a promise of a financial rebate for holidays taken in NSW.

Wran exploited the popularity of the Hawke Labor Government, elected on 5 March 1983, by stressing that a partnership between Federal and State Labor would enable NSW to reap maximum benefits from the national economic recovery that was underway. The election of a Coalition Government would jeopardise this. It was not a time to entrust the future of NSW to inexperienced amateurs. Ironically, Liberal Premier Willis had made a similar accusation against Wran in the 1976 election campaign.

Confronting the corruption issue, Wran extravagantly claimed that "our government has done more to fight crime and corruption, wherever it occurs, than any previous government in the history of NSW"[56] – admittedly, there was not much competition. Rather than addressing real issues, the Opposition was pursuing a destructive campaign that was undermining "our new national self-confidence, confidence in our democratic institutions, confidence in ourselves and each other".[57] An effective ploy was to promise that if the Government was returned it would create a Judicial Commissioner of Public Complaints to investigate allegations of wrongdoing by public office holders. The position was established but never functioned effectively and soon became defunct. It was a pale shadow of the Opposition's proposed permanent anti-crime body, which was established in 1989 as the Independent Commission Against Corruption.

Greiner launched a stinging, wide-ranging attack in his policy speech: "I will fight the Government on its record. I will fight on its failure to deal with crime and corruption. I will fight on its failure to deal with unemployment. I will fight on its record of taxes and charges. I will fight on its economic record".[58]

Aware that Wran's "Nifty Nev" image now had devious rather than glamorous connotations, the Opposition Leader said: "It may be nifty to call an election when it suits you. It may be nifty to rush around at the last minute making billion dollar promises. It may be nifty — but it isn't good government".[59] Greiner even attempted to draw a parallel between Wran and disgraced former United States President Richard Nixon. The "time for a change" theme was prominent: Labor was corrupt, had run out of ideas and lost direction. By contrast: "I promise you my government will clean up the management of NSW; that my government will give value for the State taxation dollar; that my government will tackle lawlessness, soaring crime rates, high unemployment and the plight of the aged, the sick, the disadvantaged and our children".[60]

Unlike previous campaigns, such attacks now had bite. Labor's primary vote dropped from 56 per cent to 49 per cent. The Government, however, was comfortably returned, winning 58 of the 99 seats.

Although he had won, Wran was wounded, mortally as it transpired. The old magic was gone and his appetite and enthusiasm for politics were declining. The resignation of Ferguson as Deputy Premier in February 1984 was another blow. His replacement by Ron Mulock, for whom Wran had an undeserved and inexplicable enmity, was a sign of his waning prestige in caucus. Greiner was in the ascendant in the opinion polls throughout 1985.

Corruption continued to dominate the headlines. The *Age* tapes led to the trial of Wran's close friend, High Court Judge Lionel Murphy, for attempting to pervert the course of justice. Murphy was convicted in July 1985, but acquitted at a retrial. When Murphy's retrial was announced in December 1985, Wran told the media he was convinced of Murphy's innocence. As a result, Wran was charged with contempt of court and convicted a year later. In July 1984, claims emerged that District Court Judge John Foord had attempted to influence a court case, allegedly at Wran's behest. Wran vigorously denied the charge. Foord was charged, but acquitted in September 1985. Former Chief Magistrate Murray Farquhar – reappointed at Wran's insistence in 1978 despite credible charges of close association with well-known organised crime figure George Freeman – was convicted in March 1985 of charges arising from the Street Royal Commission.[61]

Wran's previously superb judgement of situations and the electoral mood deserted him. An example was the doctors' dispute which began in 1984. Relations between the Wran Government and the medical profession had been tense during Laurie Brereton's term as Health Minister. Doctors resented his transfer of hospital resources to the western suburbs. Brereton had also passed legislation as part of the implementation of the Hawke Government's Medibank scheme that some doctors felt intruded on their professional independence. This played into the hands of the intransigent Bruce Shepherd, an orthopaedic surgeon whose aim was to dominate the medical profession. Brereton's successor, Ron Mulock, has said:

> They did not have time to mount their attack before the 1984 election, but as soon as it was over they started. Shepherd was philosophically committed to the dispute. He was also aiming to become the Federal President of the AMA and was using it as a springboard. Before all hell broke loose, I had an

hour long session with him – just the two of us in the room. He was going on about the legislative changes that Laurie Brereton had made. I was prepared to look into his concerns, but Shepherd was not amenable to compromise.[62]

In April 1984, surgeons decided to withdraw their services from public hospitals for all but emergencies. Mulock was quietly negotiating with the more reasonable sections of the profession and was close to an agreement. Then Wran stepped in:

Neville was overseas and came back just before the June ALP State conference. He asked me to meet with him and said he had decided to take the doctors on. I advised him against this: 'Neville, the game is to divide and conquer not unite them'. But he didn't listen and laid into the doctors at the Conference. On 12 June he recalled Parliament and we passed legislation with all sorts of draconian provisions, including that doctors who resigned would not be allowed back into the hospital system for seven years. Neville also threatened to bring in overseas doctors to fill the vacancies. It was like throwing petrol on the fire and it all exploded.[63]

An increasing number of surgeons offered their resignations from public hospitals, plunging the health system into crisis.

Realising that the dispute was becoming a public relations disaster, Wran backed off and said he was prepared to compromise. He left it to Mulock and Federal Health Minister Neal Blewett to sort out the mess, which they eventually did. Blewett recalled that Wran became "the biggest advocate for retreat and for calling for my head".[64] The final settlement agreed on was "so generous to the specialists [that] it pushed up health costs all over Australia".[65]

At the ALP Annual Conference at Sydney Town Hall on 7 June 1986, Wran announced his retirement. He resigned the Premiership and his seat on 4 July 1986. He had served a then record continuous term as Premier of ten years, one month and 20 days.

Enoch Powell has expressed a political truism: "All political lives, unless they are cut off in midstream at a happy juncture, end in failure, because that is the nature of politics and of human affairs".[66] Wran partly avoided that fate. He recovered enough of his old political judgment to realise that it was time to depart. To use an old Balmain expression, he was on a hiding to nothing. He bequeathed the legacy of losing office to his successor, Barrie Unsworth. Greiner won the 19 March 1988 election with 59 of the 109 seats compared to Labor's 43. There was a 10.26 per cent primary vote swing against the Government.

Graham Freudenberg, with his inimitable elegance and perspicuity, has described Wran as the voice of Sydney: "He distilled its style - its diversity and richness of character, its glamour and sophistication, its raffishness and larrikin touch, its energy and dynamism, its values of the fair-go and mateship, its cynicism, its peculiar mix of tolerance and censoriousness, its good-natured aggressiveness, its flair for the good life".[67] By mid-1986 Wran realised his time was up: "He believed he had ceased to be the true voice of Sydney, and he had lost the will to express it".[68]

Epilogue

After leaving politics, Wran had a successful career as an investment banker and businessman. According to Graham Freudenberg, he was amazed at "the sheer wealth awash around Sydney and the undeserving ease with which insiders appeared to acquire it".[69] A personal sadness in Wran's later years was the breakdown of his relationship with his wife Jill. They separated a number of times, but were finally reconciled in 2012. Suffering from dementia, Neville Wran died on 20 April 2014 at the age of 87. Over 1,500 attended his State funeral at Sydney Town Hall on 1 May.

Wran won four successive elections, two by landslides – the ALP two-party preferred vote in 1978 was 60.7 per cent and, in 1981, 58.7 per cent.[70] In terms of political, communication, administrative and parliamentary skills, he has few equals. No other NSW Premier has left as substantial a legacy of constitutional and electoral change. Wran's record of environmental, human rights and social reform is impressive. The arts received generous support under his Premiership. Basic services, such as transport, schools and hospitals, were improved. For the people of NSW, it was, on the whole, a time of economic growth, prosperity, low charges and high employment.

The major blemish on Wran's time in office is his failure to deal effectively with corruption. In answer to the question why this was so, Gary Sturgess, a senior adviser to Nick Greiner in Opposition and then Director-General of Cabinet Office when Greiner was Premier, has given a cogent explanation:

> I don't think that he was corrupt in the sense that he was taking money from business figures or colourful Sydney identities. Some of it was clearly a network of old friends whom he continued to stand by as the years progressed, such as Lionel Murphy. Some of it was that he was caught in a shift of values – things that had gone on forever like phone calls to a public official about a mate's problems were no longer acceptable. Some of it was that by the middle of the 1980s, he was forced to defend actions and decisions that he had made, and which ministers and senior public servants had taken on his watch. I suspect that he was also disinclined to believe many of the rumours, for example about Jackson. Jacko was an old rogue, and Wran knew that – but I suspect that he was appalled to discover what he'd been up to with the early release scheme.[71]

Another criticism of Wran's record is that he did not undertake the sort of public sector reforms that Greiner did, which were starting to be needed by the 1980s. Greiner recalls Wran saying to him in the mid-1990s: why did you bother with all that reform? It is hard, thankless work with no votes in it.[72]   Steketee and Cockburn have observed:

> If Wran's record in managing the State's budgets was an impressive one, the same cannot be said of his management of the State's statutory authorities. The Government, largely at Wran's urging, frequently adopted a populist rather than rational approach to the pricing policies of these authorities – decisions which have often been to the long-term disadvantage of their customers.[73]

Wran was restrained not only by political expediency, but also by a failure of imagination, in that he did not realise that the post-war public sector model was not sustainable without the post-war long boom which was ending in the 1970s and 80s.

State politics moves in ripples – a successful premier drops a stone in the pond and the ripples spread across the nation. The Wran model was the template for a new generation of Labor State premiers such as John Bannon, John Cain and Wayne Goss: reformist, competent and, above all, electorally astute.

Appendix 1

Voting in the Labor Leadership Contest 3 December 1973 as reconstructed by Rodney Cavalier

NEVILLE WRAN:

Left:

1. Ken Booth

2. Laurie Ferguson

3. Pat Flaherty

4. Merv Hunter

5. Maurie Keane

6. Keith O'Connell

7. George Petersen

8. Pat Rogan

9. Frank Walker

Ferguson acolytes:

10. Roger Degen

11. Lew Johnstone

12. Sam Jones

13. Lawrie Kelly

14. Ernie Quinn

Independent:

15. Neville Wran

Right:

16. Eric Bedford

17. Laurie Brereton

18. Terry Sheahan

PAT HILLS:

Right:

1. Gordon Barnier

2. Bill Crabtree

3. Don Day

4. Syd Einfeld

5. Richard Face

6. Lin Gordon

7. Bill Haigh

8. Pat Hills

9. Rex Jackson

10. Harry Jensen

11. Dan Mahoney

12. Cliff Mallam

13. Ron Mulock

14. George Neilly

15. Eric Ramsay

16. Jack Renshaw

17. Arthur Wade

KEVIN STEWART:

Right:

1. Brian Bannon

2. Tom Cahill

3. Peter Cox

3. Vince Durick

4. Tony Johnson

5. Nick Kearns

6. Michael Maher

8. George Paciullo

9. Kevin Stewart

Stewart preferences:

To Hills:

1. Brian Bannon

2. Tom Cahill

3. Vince Durick

4. Tony Johnson

5. Nick Kearns

To Wran:

6. Peter Cox

7. Michael Maher

8. George Paciullo

9. Kevin Stewart

Appendix 2

NSW Legislative Assembly Election Results 1973-1988

First Preference Percentages						
PARTY	1973	1976	1978	1981	1984	1988
Labor	42.9	49.8	57.8	55.7	48.8	38.5
Liberal	33.8	36.3	27.0	27.6	32.2	35.8
National	10.5	10.0	9.9	11.2	10.8	13.7
Others	12.8	3.9	5.3	5.5	8.2	12.0

Estimated Two-Party Preferred Percentage						
PARTY	1973	1976	1978	1981	1984	1988
Labor	48.4	51.6	60.7	58.7	52.5	44.0
Coalition	51.6	48.4	39.3	41.3	47.5	56.0

Seats Won						
PARTY	1973	1976	1978	1981	1984	1988
Labor	44	50	63	69	58	43
Liberal	34	30	18	14	22	39
National	18	18	17	14	15	20
Others	3	1	1	2	4	7
Total Seats	99	99	99	99	99	109

NSW Legislative Council Election Results 1978-1988

First Preference Percentages				
PARTY	1978	1981	1984	1988
Labor	54.9	51.8	46.9	37.5
Liberal	36.3	33.8	42.6	46.2
Call to Australia	..	9.1	6.1	5.7
Australian Democrats	2.8	4.0	3.2	2.7
Others	6.0	1.3	1.2	7.9

Seats Won				
PARTY	1978	1981	1984	1988
Labor	9	8	7	6
Liberal	6	5	7	7
Call to Australia	-	1	1	1
Australian Democrats	-	1	-	1
Others	15	15	15	15

Term	By-election	Date	Notes
1973-76	Coogee	20 Jul 1974	**LABOR GAIN**
	Goulburn	20 Jul 1974	Safe Country Party seat
	Lane Cove	8 Feb 1975	No Labor candidate
	Pittwater	8 Feb 1975	No Labor candidate
	Wagga Wagga	6 Dec 1975	Safe Liberal seat
	Orange	14 Feb 1976	Safe Country Party seat
1976-78	The Hills	9 Oct 1976	Safe Liberal seat
	Earlwood	15 Jul 1978	**LABOR GAIN**
1978-81	Castlereagh	23 Feb 1980	Labor retain
	Bankstown	13 Sep 1980	Labor retain
	Ku-ring-gai	13 Sep 1980	No Labor candidate
	Murray	13 Sep 1980	Safe Liberal seat
	Cessnock	21 Feb 1981	Labor retain
	Maitland	21 Feb 1981	Liberal retain
	Oxley	21 Feb 1981	Safe Country Party seat
	Sturt	21 Feb 1981	Safe Country Party seat
1981-84	Drummoyne	17 Apr 1982	Labor retain
	Kogarah	22 Oct 1983	Labor retain
	Maroubra	22 Oct 1983	Labor retain
	Marrickville	22 Oct 1983	Labor retain
	Riverstone	22 Oct 1983	Labor retain
1984-86	Murray	2 Feb 1985	No Labor candidate
	Peats	2 Feb 1985	Labor retain
	Gloucester	12 Oct 1985	No Labor candidate
	Cabramatta	1 Feb 1986	Labor retain
	Canterbury	1 Feb 1986	Labor retain
	Kiama	1 Feb 1986	Labor retain
	Pittwater	31 May 1986	No Labor candidate
	Vaucluse	31 May 1986	No Labor candidate

Source:

Antony Green, "The Wranslides and Electoral Politics" in Troy Bramston (ed.), *The Wran Era*, Federation Press, 2006.

Antony Green, "Appendix Four: Election Results 1973-1986" in Troy Bramston (ed.), *The Wran Era*, Federation Press, 2006.

Antony Green, "New South Wales By-Elections 1965-2005", NSW Parliamentary Library Research Service, Background Paper, No. 3/2005.

Antony Green, "Electing the New South Wales Legislative Council 1978 to 1995: Past Results and Future Prospects", NSW Parliamentary Library Research Service, Background Paper, No. 2/1995.

Antony Green, "Changing Boundaries, Changing Fortunes: an analysis of the NSW Elections of 1988 and 1991, NSW Parliamentary Library Research Service, Occasional Paper, No. 8, October 1998.

Notes

1   This section draws on the definitive account of Wran's early
    years, Mike Steketee and Milton Cockburn, *Wran: An Unau-
    thorised Biography*, Allen and Unwin, Sydney, 1986.

2   Quoted in Steketee and Cockburn, *Wran*, p. 43.

3   Graham Freudenberg, "Neville Kenneth Wran," in David
    Clune and Ken Turner, (eds), *The Premiers of NSW, 1856-
    2005*, Vol 2, Federation Press, Sydney, 2006, p. 402.

4   See David Clune, "Reg Downing: A Safe Pair of Hands", in
    Ken Turner and M Hogan, (eds), *The Worldly Art of Politics*,
    Federation Press, Sydney, 2006.

5   Quoted in Steketee and Cockburn, *Wran*, p. 72.

6   Rodney Cavalier, "A Case Study of Leadership Changes in
    NSW Labor, 1939-2005," in *Southern Highlands Newsletter*, No
    143, August 2008. Copy in possession of the author.

7   Cavalier, "A Case Study of Leadership Changes in NSW La-
    bor, 1939-2005".

8   Cavalier, "A Case Study of Leadership Changes in NSW La-
    bor, 1939-2005".

9   See Appendix 1 for the full details.

10 Rodney Cavalier, "What happened in 1973," in *Southern
    Highlands Newsletter*, No 144, September 2008. Copy in pos-
    session of the author.

11 Email to the author, 28.5.2020.

12 Terry Sheahan, "Reflections of a Minister," in Troy Bram-
    ston, (ed), *The Wran Era*, Federation Press, Sydney, 2006, p.
    229.

13 Brian Dale, "Glory days with Neville Wran," *Southern High-
    lands Newsletter*, No 231, January-February 2019. Copy in
    possession of the author.

14 Dale, "Glory days with Neville Wran".

15 Dale, "Glory days with Neville Wran".

16 David Clune, *Inside the Wran Era: The Ron Mulock Memoirs*,
    Connor Court, Ballan 2015, pp. 118-9.

17 Clune, *Inside the Wran Era*, pp. 118-9.

18 *Sydney Morning Herald*, 30 April 1976.

19 *Sydney Morning Herald*, 30 April 1976.

20   *Sydney Morning Herald*, 30 April 1976.

21   *Sydney Morning Herald,* 29 April 1976.

22   Brian Dale, email to the author, 23 May 2020.

23   For full details of the Wran Ministries see the NSW
      Parliamentary Record: https://www.parliament.nsw.gov.
      au/members/formermembers/Documents/Part%206%20
      combined.pdf

24   Clune, *Inside the Wran Era,* p. 137.

25   Clune, *Inside the Wran Era,* p. 132.

26   Milton Cockburn, email to author, 4 May 2020.

27   Cockburn, email to author, 4 May 2020.

28   Cockburn, email to author, 4 May 2020.

29   Rodney Cavalier, "Neville Wran (1926-2014): Eulogy
      at State Funeral," Sydney Town Hall, 1 May 2014, as
      published in *Southern Highlands Newsletter*, No 206, May
      2014.

30   Malcolm Turnbull, "How Wran was outflanked on upper
      house reform," *The Bulletin*, 14 February 1978.

31   David Clune, *Connecting with the People: The 1978 Reconstitution
      of the Legislative Council*, Legislative Council of NSW,
      History Monograph No 2, 2017.

32   Quoted in Steketee and Cockburn, *Wran*, p. 334.

33   Martin Painter, "NSW Political Chronicle, July-December
      1976," *Australian Journal of Politics and History*, Vol 23 No 1,
      April 1977, p. 80.

34   *Sydney Morning Herald*, 3 May 1978.

35   David Clune, "The State Labor Party's Electoral Record in
      Rural New South Wales 1904-1981," *Labour History*, No 47,
      November 1984.

36   Dale, "Glory days with Neville Wran".

37   Email to the author, 4 May 2020.

38   Clune, *Inside the Wran Era,* p. 136.

39   Freudenberg, in Clune and Turner, *The Premiers of NSW,* p.
      411.

40   *Sydney Morning Herald*, 13 June 1981.

41   *Sydney Morning Herald*, 25 June 1981.

42   *ALP Policy Speech, 1981 Election*, 3 September 1981.

43   *Liberal Party Policy Speech, 1981 Election*, 2 September 1981.

44   Clune, *Inside the Wran Era*, pp. 229-30.

45   Clune, *Inside the Wran Era*, p. 229.

46   On Greiner see Ian Hancock, *Nick Greiner: A Political Biography*, Connor Court, Ballan, 2013.

47   Email to the author, 24 May 2020.

48   See Russell Ross, "The Economy," in Bramston, *The Wran Era*, pp. 143-151.

49   See Alfred W McCoy, *Drug Traffic: Narcotics and Organised Crime in Australia*, Harper and Row, Sydney, 1980 and Richard Hall, *Disorganised Crime*, University of Queensland Press, St Lucia, 1986.

50   For a detailed account of these events see Steketee and Cockburn, *Wran*, pp. 294-306.

51   Brian Dale email to the author, 24 May 2020.

52   Clune, *Inside the Wran Era*, p. 228-9.

53   Clune, *Inside the Wran* Era, p. 229.

54   *Report of Commission to Inquire into New South Wales Police Administration*, 29 April 1981.

55   *Report of Special Commission of Inquiry into Certain Allegations by the Right Honourable Ian McCahon Sinclair*, January 1984; *Report of Special Commission of Inquiry into Certain Allegations by Mr. R. Bottom*, February 1984.

56   *ALP Policy Speech 1984 Election*, 13 March 1984.

57   *ALP Policy Speech 1984 Election*, 13 March 1984.

58   *Liberal Policy Speech 1984 Election*, 12 March 1984.

59   *Liberal Policy Speech 1984 Election*, 12 March 1984.

60   *Liberal Policy Speech 1984 Election*, 12 March 1984.

61   *Report of the Royal Commission of Inquiry into Certain Committal Proceedings against K.E. Humphreys*, July 1983.

62   Clune, *Inside the Wran Era*, pp. 245.

63   Clune, *Inside the Wran* Era, pp. 246.

64   Quoted in Mohamed Khadra, *Terminal Decline: A Surgeon's Diagnosis of the Australian Health Care System*, Heinemann, Melbourne, 2010.

65   Quoted in Khadra, *Terminal Decline*.

66   Enoch Powell, *Joseph Chamberlain*, Thames and Hudson, London, 1977.

67   Graham Freudenberg, "The Voice of Sydney," in Bram-

ston, *The* Wran Era, p. 99.

68   Freudenberg, in Bramston, *The Wran Era*, p. 106.

69   Freudenberg, in Clune and Turner, *The Premiers of NSW*, p. 421.

70   According to Antony Green, the only occasion on which Wran's 1978 two-party preferred result was exceeded was Barry O'Farrell's crushing 2011 Coalition victory of 64.2 per cent. Labor's highest two party preferred vote under Labor's Bob Carr was 56.2 per cent in 2003. Email to author, 7 July 2020

71   Email to the author, 13 May 2020.

72   Email to the author, 13 May 2020.

73   Steketee and Cockburn, *Wran*, p. 183.

Select bibliography

Troy Bramston, (ed), *The Wran Era*, Federation Press, Sydney, 2006.

Ernie Chaples, Helen Nelson, and Ken Turner, (eds), *The Wran Model: Electoral Politics in NSW, 1981 and 1984*, Oxford University Press, Melbourne, 1985.

Ernie Chaples, and Helen Nelson, (eds), *Case Studies in NSW Electoral Politics: A Companion Research Study to The Wran Model*, Department of Government and Public Administration, University of Sydney, 1985.

David Clune, "Elections, policy and politics: an overview," in Troy Bramston (ed), *The Wran Era*, Federation Press, 2006.

David Clune, *Connecting with the People: the 1978 Reconstitution of the Legislative Council*, Legislative Council of NSW, History Monograph No 2, 2017.

David Clune, (with J Upton), *Inside the Wran Era: The Ron Mulock Memoirs*, Connor Court, Ballan, 2015.

David Clune, and Gareth Griffith, *Decision and Deliberation: The Parliament of NSW, 1856-2003*, Federation Press, Sydney, 2005.

David Clune, and Ken Turner, "1973," in Michael Hogan, and David Clune, (eds), *The People's Choice: Electoral Politics in Twentieth Century NSW*, Sydney University and NSW Parliament, Sydney, Vol 3, 2001.

Brian Dale, *Ascent to Power: Wran and the Media*, Allen and Unwin, Sydney, 1985.

Graham Freudenberg, *Cause for Power: The Official History of the NSW Branch of the Australian Labor Party*, Pluto Press, Sydney, 1991.

Graham Freudenberg, "Neville Kenneth Wran," in David Clune and Ken Turner, (eds), *The Premiers of NSW, 1856-2005*, 2 vols, Federation Press, Sydney, 2006.

Jim Hagan, and Ken Turner, *A History of the Labor Party in NSW, 1891-1991*, Longman Cheshire, Melbourne, 1991.

Ian Hancock, *Nick Greiner: A Political Biography*, Connor Court, Ballan, 2013.

Michael Hogan and David Clune, (eds), *The People's Choice: Electoral Politics in Twentieth Century NSW*, Sydney University and New South Wales Parliament, Sydney, Vol 3, 2001.

Mike Steketee and Milton Cockburn, *Wran: An Unauthorised Biography*, Allen and Unwin, Sydney, 1986.

Neville Wran